My Father Says Grace

My Father Says Grace

Poems by Donald Platt

The University of Arkansas Press
Fayetteville
2007

Copyright © 2007 by The University of Arkansas Press

All rights reserved
Manufactured in the United States of America

ISBN-10: 1-55728-837-2
ISBN-13: 978-1-55728-837-0

11   10   09   08   07   5   4   3   2   1

Designed by Liz Lester

♾ The paper used in this publication meets the minimum requirements of
the American National Standard for Permanence of Paper for Printed
Library Materials Z39.48-1984.

LIBRARY OF CONGRESS CATALOGING-IN-PUBLICATION DATA

Platt, Donald, 1957–
       My father says grace : poems / by Donald Platt.
              p.   cm.
       ISBN 1-55728-837-2 (pbk. : alk. paper)
       I. Title.
       PS3566.L286M95   2007
       811'.54—dc22

                                  2006031457

for my father

ACKNOWLEDGMENTS

The author gratefully thanks the editors of the following publications, in which these poems first appeared:

AGNI: "Cartwheels," "Red Door"; *Alaska Quarterly Review:* "Compass Rose," "Sundowning Exit-Seeker"; *Black Warrior Review:* "After" (reprinted at www.versedaily.org); *BOMB:* "Turtle with the World on Its Back"; *Colorado Review:* "Treble and Treble and Back"; *Crazyhorse:* "Joy"; *Field:* "Snapshot"; *Georgia Review:* "Ash Wednesday," "Mirage," "My Father Says Grace"; *Iowa Review:* "Two Poets Meet"; *Kenyon Review:* "Setting Sun"; *Michigan Quarterly Review:* "Andantino Cantabile with Double Rainbow"; *Poetry Northwest:* "Sizzling Happy Family," "Summer Arrhythmias"; *Shenandoah:* "For Janis Joplin with Pink Feather Boa in the Clouds at the Edge of the Atlantic Ocean"; *Southern Review:* "Amazing Grace Beauty Salon," "Ground Transport," "Killing the Minotaur," "Name & Address," "Victor Talking Machine Co."; *Southwest Review:* "Pretty Boy, Rifle Barrels, Carnations"; *Virginia Quarterly Review:* "Brother Death, Sister Life," "Walt Whitman Wrestling Naked with the Young Trees."

"Brother Death, Sister Life" was reprinted in *The Pushcart Prize XXIX* (2005). "Two Poets Meet" was anthologized in *The Best American Poetry, 2006*.

Thanks to the Ragdale Foundation for a residency and to Purdue University for a Research Foundation Summer Faculty Grant, a Center for Creative Endeavors Grant, and various reductions in teaching responsibilities, all of which were essential to the writing of these poems. Thanks to Enid Shomer for selecting this book for publication in the University of Arkansas Press's Poetry Series. The author is profoundly grateful to Bruce Beasley, Daniel Corrie, and Dana Roeser for their comments on drafts of these poems and on the book manuscript. As always, he is indebted to his family—Dana Roeser, Eleanor and Lucy Platt, and Martha, Donald, and Michael Platt—for their love and support.

CONTENTS

Sizzling Happy Family   *3*

Joy   *6*

My Father Says Grace   *8*

Brother Death, Sister Life   *11*

Ash Wednesday   *17*

Summer Arrhythmias   *20*

Turtle with the World on Its Back   *22*

Compass Rose   *25*

Treble and Treble and Back   *35*

Killing the Minotaur   *38*

Mirage   *42*

Victor Talking Machine Co.   *44*

Sundowning Exit-Seeker   *49*

Name & Address   *53*

Walt Whitman Wrestling Naked with the Young Trees   *55*

After   *58*

For Janis Joplin with Pink Feather Boa in the Clouds
   at the Edge of the Atlantic Ocean   *60*

Pretty Boy, Rifle Barrels, Carnations   *65*

Setting Sun   *69*

Snapshot   *73*

Andantino Cantabile with Double Rainbow   *74*

Cartwheels   *77*

Amazing Grace Beauty Salon   *80*

Two Poets Meet   *84*

Red Door   *86*

Ground Transport   *90*

My Father Says Grace

Sizzling Happy Family

The mother and father
who brought me into this life on the cusp of the Crab and the Lion
now forget

to eat. They line up their dozens of pills on the formica
counter and swallow them
with over-diluted orange juice concentrate. When we visit, I find nothing

for dinner but three frozen chicken
pot pies. I take my two children grocery-shopping and cook for all of us
my own bastard version of Sizzling

Happy Family, that ancient Chinese meal of pork, chicken, beef, and seafood
grilled together
with vegetables. My wife and I eat no meat, so I sauté tiger shrimp and garlic,

scallops, squid,
summer squash, red peppers, asparagus, snow peas, and Maine
mussels with bunches

of cilantro and purple basil chopped. I season it with coarse sea salt
and fresh
ground pepper, and serve it with a pyramid of corn on the cob picked

that day. My mother
and father stare at this steaming platter of smells and colors
harvested from the earth

and ocean, cooked for them in desperation and hunger
by one of their two
middle-aged sons. Slowly, tentatively, they help

themselves
to this strange food. My mother picks up a mussel in its shell
steamed open

like an iris in late April to reveal its blue-and-white-enameled
inner petals.
She teases out the plump sexual meat and chews its tender

saltiness. My father
reaches for the corn, then spears asparagus and shrimp together
on the tines

of his trembling fork. "Remember," he turns to my mother, "Napoli,
that little trattoria
where we ate linguini with artichoke hearts, and how we saw

octopi hung on clotheslines
with the day's wash?" My mother holds up a sunburst of squid
like a wild wedding ring

and stuffs it whole into her mouth. "Yes," she replies, "and the red table wine
cheap as water
and us on Pegasus, our Harley, cruising down the Costa Brava

after the war
past the entire Third Army on maneuvers, all those catcalls!" They laugh
together and have forgotten

us. Sixty years slip like an avalanche from their shoulders. It is
another country.
They live on kisses and calamari, tasting everything

the waiter puts
before them—seviche, its raw scallops, onions, and green peppers
over which my father squeezes

lime juice bright and astringent as sunlight, then fritto misto. Keep eating,
I want to tell them. Remember
how hungry you are for all of this. Belch. Throw down the napkins

stained with the prints
of your lips. Order coffee and the pears with rum. Have them flame it.
Don't leave the table. Not yet.

Joy

Joy is the jumbo
purple balloon my daughter Eleanor blows her small lungfuls
of life into, and then

throws to me, her stupid father who has forgotten
how to laugh.
The game is not to let joy touch the ground but pass

it on to someone
else—I hit it with one loose fist across the room to Michael my brother
who at forty,

with one chromosome too many and lousy fine motor coordination,
can still catch the slow
thin-skinned balloon, chortle, jerk his head, as if whiplashed

in an invisible
car crash, and toss it to our question-mark-backed father.
Dad can't remember

what day it is or where he lives, laughs and bats it on
to my mother,
whose shatterproof face has crazed into a thousand

flaws. Her pacemaker
needs a new battery, but she giggles and slaps
the balloon back

to me. I'm grinning, then guffawing at our spasmodic
            juggling act,
five people, three generations gyrating together, straining toward

            a globe that glows
and floats over our heads, this weightless thing no more than a cubic foot
            of breath, about to break.

My Father Says Grace

What did my father
think he was saying the night he had his stroke
but didn't know it

and stood over the warmed-up leftover meatloaf
congealing in its grease
to give thanks for such bounty as they were

about to receive?
When he spoke the holy words, nothing
but the jangled

syllables of aphasia came from his God-struck tongue,
and my awed mother
and retarded brother listened harder than they ever had

to any of his Sunday sermons
or cocktail tirades to try to understand the message
God had given him

and him alone. Was it *Blessed be the animals that die*
so we may live?
Or *Bless the mud and straw under their hooves*

and the feed grain
they root for there? Or *Everything that eats must be eaten.*
Bless the dung

squeezed out by the pink flowers of the sows' anuses
for we ourselves
must be digested in the gut of the earth. No part or particle of us

is ever

wasted? "Utter gibberish," my mother exclaimed later, drawing
             circles with a forefinger

in the air around her right ear and smiling
             so as not
to weep. "His fuses all blown!" Maybe he was saying, *Praise be*

             to the salt
in its shaker for it brings out the true taste of whatever
             we eat. We are

its savor. The daily task God gives to the dead
             is to count
its unnumberable crystals and to write the history

             of the world
on each of its grains, dissolve them in a glass of water, and drink
             it all down.

Its taste is the taste of the Dead Sea. No salt shall season or preserve
             our words.
Did the fresh-cut zinnias on the dinner table listen

             to his crazy
rantings and bow down? The sounds that keep coming out of his mouth
             mean less than nothing,

but I listen to the silence behind his miswired phonemes
             and try again
to translate his tongue's rustlings. *Glory be,* says the silence,

to the blood clot
that travels the left hemisphere of the brain like a coin
in a slot machine.

Death is the jackpot. Glory be to the carotid artery
whose blood
no longer reaches the cerebellum. Glory be to the body, switchboard

that will finally
shut down. All glory to nothing, nowhere, and no one
as it was

in the beginning before we were born. My father keeps jabbering
until my mother
takes him by the hand and tells him it's time

to lie down. He quiets,
sits, and stammers out the two words left us at our end.
It's *Thanks,* then *Amen.*

Brother Death, Sister Life

Laudato si', mi Signore, per sora nostra Morte corporale
da la quale nullo omo vivente po' scampare.
                                                —ST. FRANCIS

            Death is my idiot
brother, who comes babbling something I don't yet
            understand and throws

his arms around me and kisses me full
            on the mouth.
I hug him back. St. Francis got it all

            wrong. Death
isn't our sister, *Laudato si', mi Signore.*
            Tom Andrews

knew it too. Death was always his brother,
            John, who kept
beckoning him from the beyond. "The dead drag

            a grappling hook
for the living. The hook is enormous," Tom said
            in his shortest

poem. Tom was the hooked rainbow trout fighting
            hard, prismatic
flash of silver muscle breaking the surface, taking the line out

            from the screeching
reel with the drag on, and finally hauled thrashing into the air, gasping
            for water.

Death was his true element. He swam well. Life caught him,
                    then threw
him back. *Laudato si', mi Signore.* He almost jumped

                    from a seven-story
parking garage, while his poetry students waited for him
                    to come

to the last class of the year. The tulips bloomed late,
                    as always
in Indiana, recalcitrant miserly spring that spent

                    only a handful
of red petals, when it should have been prodigal
                    April. Tom walked

back down. *Laudato si', mi Signore.* Did he teach
                    that last class?
I never learned. A year later he visited us in Georgia and told us how

                    one week earlier
he had piped his exhaust into the cab of the blue truck with a rubber hose
                    but stopped

when his kittens Geoffrey and Emma crawled
                    onto the windshield
and tried to climb in with him, mewing for milk, scrambling up the glass

                    and sliding
back down. When he finally went to bed, Dana and I worried
                    he would kill

himself overnight. But then, at the same moment, we burst
            out laughing—
Tom was too "polite" to commit suicide

            at his friends' house.
Laudato si', mi Signore. The forsythia flamed
            like a guardian

angel with a drawn sword outside his window
            while he slept
sound. Chronic depression couldn't kill him. His hemophilia

            didn't stop
him riding motorcycles down the long flat roads of Indiana
            through cornfields

that stretched dark green to the horizon, so much sky,
            a few golden tassels
of cirrus clouds, the sun setting within reach

            on one side,
the full moon rising on the other, those two shining brass
            pans of the invisible

balance that seesaws and weighs out our nights and days. Into the humid dusk
            Tom cruised
at seventy miles per hour. His girlfriends held on tight. *Laudato si',*

            mi Signore.
They were all at his funeral, four ex-girl friends, two ex-fiancées,
            and Carrie

his ex-wife. They sobbed and embraced each other in chorus.
           His old teacher and I
read five of his poems aloud and then shut the words

                 back in their books.
The pianist played Satie's *Gymnopédie* while sirens
                 careened

past the church. Tom, you would have loved the clanging fire engine
                 that interrupted
the program so that the pianist had to stop

                 and wait
for all that commotion to pass. We sang "Ye Watchers and Ye Holy Ones."
           It took a long name, thrombotic

thrombocytopenic purpura—freak virus, "a rare, but sometimes deadly,
                 blood disorder"—to kill you,
and five weeks in a coma while Alice your mother and Alice your fiancée tried

                 to keep you
alive. Your brother, who died from renal failure twenty-one years
                 ago, kept whispering

through your respirator's deep kiss, telling you not
                 to be afraid—
"It must be a country without pain. It must be a quiet

                 place where the stillness
under your wrist is entered like a field of thyme
                 and peppergrass. . . ."

Laudato si', mi Signore. Today, at my parents' summer cottage,
    my own brother yanks
me by the hand and points to the forty-foot silver birches

        uprooted and blown down
by an August storm's microbursts. "Where baz, baz?" he lisps.
        "Buds?" I ask.

He jerks his head from side to side. I try again.
        "Birds?"
He smiles and nods. He means the crows, whose black song wakes

        him every morning,
have had to leave the birches and have flown to roost in the jack pines. *Awe,*
        awe, they cry. Grief

is the only note they know. *Laudato si', mi Signore.* How I'll remember
        Tom Andrews always
is in my friend's story at the bar after the funeral—

        him flying down
the hill past her house, doing a handstand on her son Will's
        skateboard, while

she stood petrified on her front porch with beautiful Carrie, who shouted
        out only,
"Hey you, crazed bleeder jock on that skateboard,

        wanna get married?"
In the bar, eleven years later, Carrie blushed. It was her, Sister Life,
        Tom courted

upside down, feet pointing to the sky, his body a swaying
exclamation
point, the skateboard beneath him rumbling hallelujah

over the pitted
asphalt, while Carrie clapped, whistled, and called after him, "Come back,
you dummkopf. Come back!"

Ash Wednesday

I reach out my hand to dip fingertips
into the holy water, but find the font

empty except for a handful of smooth
speckled stones. I touch them and sign myself

with a cross of air. Yesterday Jennie
telephoned to tell me that my brother

has blood in his stool. I talked to Michael
and asked him how his stomach felt. But he,

born with Down syndrome, will say only *Yes*
on the telephone. What does Jennie give you

to eat? *Yes.* Were you afraid at the doctor's
office? *Yes.* When did you first see the blood

in the toilet? *Yes.* Do you still have pain
in your gut? *Yes.* What time of day does it get

worse? *Yes.* To have one word for everything
in the world, one monosyllable like

a smooth stone that you keep clenched in your hand.
Not Molly Bloom's breathless *yes*—"would I yes

to say yes my mountain flower and first I
put my arms around him yes"—but never-

theless your own *yes*. And when someone speaks
to you, you open your fist and show him

the one stone, moist with your sweat. It lies still
in your palm, an egg. It will hatch no bird

to wing its blue flash from bare tree to bare
tree in early March, or sing three clear notes,

a small ascending scale of praise, one phrase
or question repeated at intervals throughout

the white syntax of our unpunctuated
days, in which I wake to be bedazzled by

frost ferns etched with a diamond burin
on our windows and more new snow. Brother,

you are my oracle. I bring you questions
that have no human answers. Why does beauty

exist next to pain? Why does nothingness
shine so blindingly and have the cold blue glint

of unfathomable sky? How can our feet
keep walking here, breaking through the ice crust

into the deep down of powder beneath it?
Our boots make the sound of breaking glass. We

stomp and jump for the sheer pleasure of hearing
the crust crunch and crack. We kick up snow. Why

are we, as Gerard Manley Hopkins said,
such soft sift and drift in a smashed hourglass?

How can the sky keep dropping blue feathers
from its hovering steady wings, which we

stoop to pick up and hold, single blue flames
cupped in our cold hands? Why do the frost ferns

flower, flash, flicker, and finally melt
to rain on our window panes? The priest signs

my forehead with ashes that have been blessed
and sprinkled with holy water. *Rend your hearts,*

not your raiment, says today's lesson from
the Old Testament. Brother, my heart is rent

with what I don't have metaphors for. Why were
you born with a rock in your throat? Why will

you die while I breathe in and out? Are words
blood money I must pay? *Yes* is all you say.

Summer Arrhythmias

Weak heart, fist knocking on a door that doesn't open,
        have patience.
Keep banging against my ribs. One early afternoon or late summer

        night that has already
been recorded in a hospital chart, God will swing the door
        wide. At first

you won't know what to do. You will stand there
        foolishly knocking
on nothing. The blood slows to a shuffle

        from atrium
to ventricle in its felt slippers and hushes along the starlit
        arteries. Death

is our neighbor. Do you come here to borrow a cup of flour,
        some sugar, an egg?
Stand there on the worn threshold over which

        everyone passes. Outside
the crickets are a digital clock's small alarm. Dawn comes with its crimson
        lipstick streaks. Stars

dissolve. The sky opens its one gold-lidded
        bloodshot eye.
Step through. Leave the body. It has been good,

all of it—
both the pleasure and the pain you, stammering heart, have given and received
though not

in equal measures. It doesn't matter. Now, shorn one, you must learn to fly.
Who will wear the paper
wings my daughter once constructed in kindergarten and gave me

as a birthday gift? They have purple
and yellow stripes and resemble the blades of oars. They got torn. They won't
lift me up

in this air I row through now. The only way to go is in and down
and out.
Heart, you keep hopping like a toad before the power mower.

Turtle with the World on Its Back

Small turtle
sculpted out of sandstone, curio come all the way from Bolivia,
        given to us by a friend

who told me that there on Tuesdays and Thursdays the farmers
        and cattle ranchers
pour tequila over your shell and say a prayer

        before they drink,
how can you carry the world on your back? The oldest myths
        agree that you stagger

slowly through the mud because you bear the whole flat earth
        and the firmament's
frog spawn of stars on your humped shell. Some of your brethren, the giant

        Galapagos tortoises,
live twice as long as we do. Bubba and Clarence, stubborn 500-pounders
        on "breeding loan" to the L.A. Zoo,

were hatched in 1925, the same year that my mother-in-law, Daingerfield
        Davis Roeser,
now slowly dying of lung cancer, was born. They will

        outlive her
by decades. Little turtle, icon of everlastingness, it's Saturday night.
        I'm almost exactly a quarter

of the age of the oldest living tortoise, estimated to be
                    one hundred and seventy-two
years old. Happy birthday, all crawling things! I'm going to go out

                    in our backyard,
sit in the rusted iron lawn chair, and get good and shit-faced
                    under the harvest

moon. The college kids next door are partying hard.
                    They laugh, shout, and throw
water balloons at each other so that the nipples of the women

                    in their white T-shirts
show dark and taut through the wet fabric. What do they know
                    of living and dying?

Nothing yet. They're too drunk to notice me, middle-aged
                    dirty old man,
ogling them in the dusk. I set you, my stone box turtle,

                    down in the sparse damp grass
and pour the whole of my first bottle of beer over your domed
                    back. It pools

and turns the dirt to yeasty, hop-scented mud. I dip
                    my finger there
and draw one smear across my wrinkled tortoise

forehead. What prayer
shall I make out of such mud? God, visible only in the phases of the moon
that changes from

thumbnail paring to the fanlight of half a lemon slice to one
of the gibbous golden onion
domes of the Kremlin and, finally, to a round brass subway token

sliding into night's
turnstile slot, let my mother-in-law die quickly and with no more
pain. The beer

scours the back of my throat. Slow altocumulus clouds are wood grain
that the moonlight
polishes to a high silver sheen. I touch the sections of the turtle's

scarred stone shell,
its braille, indecipherable swirls and hieroglyphs, a language
I must go blind to learn.

Compass Rose

For my mother-in-law, Daingerfield Davis Roeser
(1925–2002)

NORTH

"A spot on the lungs," and a new country
opens before you. The doctor's words clear

the sky. Wind is a blackboard eraser
wiping the cloud nouns back to blue nowhere.

Ten degrees. After the leaves fall, there is
more sky. Learn here to read what lasts. Bare trees

scrawl the letters of their gnarled alphabets.
The teacher let me clean the erasers

at recess. I clapped them together, felt
cymbals, mute music, chalk dust I breathed in.

NORTHEAST

In the house I grew up in, the windows
had bubbles. Some were the size of the fizz

in flutes of brut champagne. A steady stream
that rose to explode on my upper lip.

Others were clear blisters, which held the air
people were breathing in the mid-eighteen

hundreds. I wanted to pop the bubbles
and breathe that older, colder air. One was

the size of a microscope's peephole. I
shut one eye, looked through it with the other,

and saw the world warp—shriveled crab-apple
globes swirled into blood gouts on a black branch

against snow, leopard gules and rampant, bend
sinister, white escutcheon of nothing.

EAST

While she is doing dying's slow inch work
and the doctor orders more CAT scans and

radiation, I split wood near the cold
spring equinox, Canaan, Connecticut.

To be outside of time and place. To be
nowhere. Here I concentrate on the axe,

on swinging it down in a perfect arc
whose center is the point where my sternum

and clavicle meet, on finding the right
angle to split the hardwood asunder

and open what grew slowly in the dark,
its raw ripped grain, an inner aurora

borealis of the quickening mind,
concentric circles of the sun beneath

bark. What the whetted axe says as it thunks
again into the seasoned chopping block

is equinox, equinox, equinox.
Crocus spoken out of the frozen ground.

SOUTHEAST

One day I too will leave it all behind.
The Chock-Full-O'-Nuts coffee can brimming

with nails, screws, wing nuts. A basket you wove
from supple cane switches, meant to hold eggs

warm from the fat brood hen. That green hose coiled
in the shade by your mulched beds, the always-

about-to-strike snake of invisible
water, fifty-five pounds of pressure per

square inch, held back by the nozzle's trigger
finger, the spigot left on. April comes

and goes. Some days your hands are knotted pain.
They worked the soil and made hydrangeas bloom,

azaleas, gardenias, and sweet peas.
Outside, on the wrought-iron chair, I see

a sweat-stiffened leather gardening glove
that still holds the shape of your closing hand.

SOUTH

Over your cell phone, the hiss and backwash
of each strained breath. "I don't need a second

damn opinion." Your diagnosis is
some unpronounceable carcinoma,

stage IV, both lungs. "Weeks," the sole prognosis.
Magnolias open their supernovas

among the dark green leaves. A seam of ants
crawls across the creamy blossom. You see

everything for the first time because
it has become the last time. The solstice

holds us in its interminable light.
A hummingbird hovers the bergamot,

its wings vibrate eighty times per second.
Seventy years turn to iridescence.

SOUTHWEST

The place *where neither moss nor rust corrupts,*
where thieves do not break through and steal, exists

not behind some dead-bolted door, but here
at the center of the wilting desert

rose, whose outer petals turn almost black.
My fingers crumble them into a bowl

for potpourri, *she loves me, she loves me
not,* until I come to the inner red

velvet vellum plush of living petals
beneath the desiccated ones, faint smell

of must and green perfume, the day distilled
to two small words, *I am, I am.* Outside,

Carolyn Hall, my wife's old friend, waters
hot peppers, diagnosed twelve years ago

with lymphoma. *I am, I am.* Six months
were all the doctors gave her. Chili pods

dried, sliced open, and the seeds sautéed
in cold-pressed, extra-virgin olive oil

until our eyes sting and water. *I am,
I am.* Essence of sun and dirt is all

we are at best. Because the nozzle leaks,
a cuff of water curls around her wrist,

cool sleeve of seamless everlastingness.
Lizard's tongue, quick as lightning, licks the air.

WEST

Tethered like a dog to her oxygen
tank by twenty feet of thin clear tubing,

my mother-in-law has traveled the world,
which is now reduced to one chair, one bed.

She waits for the movers to come and pack
up the house. Coughing for each breath, hacking

like a jackhammer, she must keep going
up and up into death's thinner air with

no way down. Soon she will reach the summit,
stand still, and see three hundred and sixty

degrees, immeasurable blue distance,
mountains' groundswell, rough chop in the middle

of the Pacific. She remembers when
she was a carsick child in the back seat

of their black Buick and her stepmother
pointed out the green sweep of terraced hills.

"What are terrorist hills?" she had asked. Now
she must travel these badlands without her

oxygen. She sees clearly the mother
who abandoned her, who on their last day

together wore a white muslin dress, scent
of lavender. Her mother is bending

close to kiss her, and she shouts, "No, I hate
you. Go away!" And then she comes back to

the bare room, to faces she should know, to
someone stooping over her and giving

her a glass of ice water. Is it her
own daughter? Are the movers here at last?

NORTHWEST

Yesterday you were cremated. The wind
comes out of the northwest with light rain. Men

in wet yellow hard hats slowly lower
concrete pipes suspended by swaying chains

from the meat hook of an orange crane down
into the gouged, muddy, six-foot ditch. They

are laying a wastewater main. Who will
scatter your ashes above the high-tide

line at Cape May Point, those low dunes you used
to walk along? Your husband and younger

son will go there alone, dig a shallow
trench that measures one body length, shake ashes,

coarse as stone-ground corn meal, from a tin can.
While Douglas watches, Erwin will cover

the trough with sand. When he has brushed the last
grains back over you, he will howl once, cry

out your name. The sun opens and shuts like
a clam shell. Surf makes the noise of rending

metal. The sea slides in and out on its
slick ball bearings. You are here and nowhere.

TRUE NORTH

The first hurricane will wash your ashes
away. You'll be swept south past Diamond Shoals,

whose soundings cannot be charted because
their sands keep shifting. No map will tell us

in what whirlpool-potholed five-knot riptide
you've dissolved. Where is true north? Compasses

spin wild. You will go beyond Ocracoke
Island, past Cape Fear and Frying Pan Shoals,

through shallow waters full of shipwrecks and
unexploded ordnance. You will pass through

the mouths of moray eels. One with the surge
and silt, you will be continually

translated. You are the compass rose's
eight petals in which all directions meet.

HERE

I stand in front of the raised beds of roses,
dumbly touch their torn, tissue-paper petals,

origami that no human hand can fold,
velvety vermillions, yellows tinged with blush

along their edges, salmons, creams, each hybrid
labeled with a metal nameplate stuck into

the dirt at its roots. *Chrysler Imperial,*
Queen Elizabeth, Bishop Darlington, Peace,

I recite the names of the roses to ease
my mind full-blown with grief. On a single bush

I see together the unopened buds like
infants' uncircumcised penises, full blooms

as big as small cabbages, and the wilting
heads with their disheveled petals. *Paradise,*

Shreveport, Summer Dream. It's over so quickly.
The day before she died, my mother-in-law,

who could no longer speak, scrawled out her last words:
"I'm better. Cannot exert. Go out & play."

The next day her older son, to whom she had
given power of attorney, bent his head

down to hers, hair spread out upon the pillow
like the rays of a gray sun in a drawing

by a child, and then told her that they had signed
the deed over, sold the old house. She nodded

and died. *Gene Boener, Rubens, French Lace, Honor.*
A black woman, pushing an old white woman

in her wheelchair out for air, stops and points at
a squirrel, brown rat with a feather boa

curled over its back like a question mark. It's
eating red-orange petals. "Well, I never

seen a squirrel eat no rose before. That's a
first. Look at how his mouth is all red." We stare.

The squirrel scares, literally "hightails" it
up a scrub pine. A woman with a walker

comes and buries her wrinkled, made-up face deep
in Mister Lincoln's big, luxurious blooms,

breathes in their scent. "That's the best," she says. "He's just
a doll." I can smell their perfume from three feet

away. It mixes with the salt onshore breeze.
Fragrant Cloud, Double Delight, Mister Lincoln.

Treble and Treble and Back

"Stamp, step, and treble,
hop back, and treble one-two, step, cut, and one-two-three,
up, down, and treble one-two."

My daughter and her friend Jessica chant their dance steps
in unison
to make the flat cornfields of Indiana pass faster

as I drive them
at eighty miles per hour to their Irish dance class on the south side
of Indy. Nothing

else to do, I tune in a staticky FM station
that fades out
and in. "Tora Bora . . . 155-millimeter howitzers . . . the will of Allah . . .

carpet-bombing . . . no water. . . ."
The words of a war mix with the girls' dance steps, and I think of the crowds
in Kabul dancing

in the streets to music, which had been outlawed for ten years,
now broadcast
over the PA system—was it the wavering flute

notes of the desert
dervishes, two-thousand-years old, or Western-style shake,
rattle, and roll?

Does the chain-saw music of the B-52s change pitch
after they've dropped
their hundred-ton payloads? Listen to the drone of the zither

and the fighter jets
strafing the retreat routes, breaking the sound barrier when
their afterburners

kick in. It's "heel step and heel step and toe click
and down."
My daughter's steel-toed hard shoes will hammer

out their own rhythms
on the scored plywood of the practice floor. "Dance faster!"
her teacher, a former

world champion, yells. "Memorize your steps until your feet
know them cold
and you don't have to think." I shut off the radio.

What is the music
of this driven world? Here it's all eighteen-wheelers
with the throttle

wide open. Their spinning chrome hubcaps reflect
miles on miles
of plowed-under fields with a few stalks of corn stubble glinting raggedly

in late December light.
The westering wheels whine a high-pitched plainsong. Theirs is the litany
of commerce:

Cleveland Contract Carriers, Piazza Produce / Wholesale Fruit
& Vegetables,
Continental Express, Caution Wide Turns. These transport trucks,

forty tons when packed full,
bring their cargoes to loading docks marked Shipping & Receiving.
What do they ship?

What do we receive? The world gives us its goods and its troubles.
My daughter must dance
it all over and over until her feet no longer stumble

through the split-second
cross-steps and "slide two-three, step up, click down, and treble
and treble and back."

Killing the Minotaur

Why must we keep reliving the old myths? I didn't remember Theseus
　　　　worming his way
through the maze and unwinding the white thread

　　　　　from a girl's spool
to return to daylight after killing with bare hands a bellowing man
　　　　who wore a bull's head,

but there I was, snaking electrical wire through the crawl space
　　　　　of the rich man's
dream house on the top of Buck's Elbow, temp work

　　　　the summer I turned
twenty-three. The living room was going to be a turquoise-tiled pool
　　　　so he could float

free of our ordinary working life and look through glass walls out over
　　　　　the green valley crisscrossed
with concrete where he had developed shopping malls. It wasn't Crete,

　　　　and the bald rich man,
whose name I forget, wasn't Minos. He gave the whole crew Miller High Lifes
　　　　and showed us how his Airedale, Hughie,

could catch a frisbee. When the foreman asked for volunteers to string wire
　　　　under the floorboards,
no one moved, and gradually everyone's gaze swiveled around

　　　　to me. I was the one
temp guy. The foreman told me, "Watch out for rattlesnakes."
　　　　It wasn't a joke. I had seen

dozens of them sunning on the flat rocks around the house. They gave me
                    a coil of Romex cable
and a flashlight, and I crawled through the dirt, every nerve tuned

                    for the frantic
high-pitched rattle, ready to wriggle backwards like a nimble
                    hermit crab.

I breathed the dust my knees scuffed up. My head hit the floor's two-by-tens.
                    The trapped air was hot.
My flashlight went dim. I almost screamed when a rat

                    brushed my thigh.
I was tunneling through bad dreams down toward my father,
                    the king diamondback

in whose coiled silence I had lived, waiting for the sudden
                    unpredictable strike
of his disapproval—"What do you mean you want to write

                    poems? They won't
get you anywhere." I kept going, unreeling the cable like umbilical
                    cord, shouldering

down some black birth canal. I got lucky. I never came face-to-face
                    with the Minotaur.
We give the old myths our new breath. When I came out

                    smeared with red clay and sweat,
everyone laughed. Then we heard it, the dog's warning bark
                    and the high whine

of the rattle that cut the humid air like a band saw switched
                    suddenly on.
We ran down the driveway and saw the coiled, gray-and-black length of it,

                    thick as a man's wrist,
its vibrating tail, and Hughie the Airedale circling, magnetized, all
                    instinct. The dog

lunged, and the snake struck him three times fast as the young
                    Muhammad Ali
hit Sonny Liston, but the dog kept going and grabbed

                    the snake in his jaws
just behind its head and shook it hard, whipping
                    it back and forth

to break its back. Bits of rattle and snake guts
                    rained on the driveway.
We cheered. When the foreman stretched the limp diamondback

                    out with his shovel,
it measured eight-and-a-half feet, longer than any mortal. The rich man
                    drove Hughie in the front seat

like a hero down the switchback mountain road to the vet's.
                    "He'll be OK," the foreman said.
"Dogs don't take snakebite bad as humans." Years later, I heard

                    how the rich man—
his name was Yarborough—blew his brains out the next summer
                    with a shotgun

in the living room that was a swimming pool. On the first anniversary
of his death,
his wife put a handgun in her mouth and angled the barrel awkwardly up

against her hard palate.
Their one son found both of them. The Minotaur lives somewhere in the coils
of the cortex and gnaws

his way out of our skulls. If I kill the Minotaur, I kill myself. My father's
depressions filled our house
for years with invisible smoke that made all our eyes water. I couldn't

breathe. Theseus forgot
to change the black sails to white. Believing his son dead, the aging father
threw himself off a cliff.

Father, Minotaur, old diamondback, I carry the two mute vertebrae of broken
rattle I picked up like dice
and still keep in my pocket. All day long I finger them. They sing.

Mirage

Because my mother's eyes have been failing from gradually
        progressing
glaucoma, she doesn't see the dust that shrouds

      all the mirrors in her house
with its fine gray veil. I look into the two hazy oval mirrors
        that gaze down

over my parents' double dresser from their frames
        of bird's-eye
maple. Sunk deep in their silver shallows,

      a woman
combs her wavy auburn hair and rubs cold cream into
        her smooth

cheeks, which will slowly erode to old age's arroyos, waiting
        for the winter
rains to fill and flood the dry washes. A man adjusts

      his loud tie,
carefully tightening its noose. He kisses her neck and hands her
        from behind his back

a pink rose freaked with yellow, which she puts in a bud vase
        before the mirrors, where
its wilting flame becomes doubled, then gutters. Two brothers sneak

into their parents'
bedroom and jump up and down on the forbidden bed
in weightless

ecstasy. The boy I once was stands naked and holds up his mother's
hand mirror
to the larger mirrors, so that he can see what his back and buttocks

look like,
the secret cleft, those two globes like the flesh of a flushed, silvery
peach. We are

dust on the surface of an old mirror. What hand will wipe it clean
and clear
to reveal ourselves to ourselves, ripples rising from the black asphalt's heat?

Victor Talking Machine Co.

I turn the old Victrola's crank until the inner spring's wound
 tight, about
to snap, then swing the chrome-plated arm shaped like a muzzle-loading pistol

 and ease the steel needle
down on the black grooves of a 78. The machine crackles.
 I open wide

the wooden cabinet doors and "Caro Nome" pours
 in Amelita Galli-Curci's
scratchy velvet voluptuous voice over the tables of the tag sale,

 over cheap, imitation cut-glass
bowls, springform pans, potato mashers, golf clubs, bad art prints,
 over Degas's catatonic

absinthe drinker with her silver, cake-like hat trimmed with black fur.
 Galli-Curci's coloratura
floats its slur of high Bs, helium balloons a child lets go,

 above our lives'
accumulated junk and bric-a-brac. *Col pensier il mio desir   A te sempre volerà,
 E fin l'ultimo*

mio sospir,   Caro nome, tuo sarà. "In my thoughts, desire shall fly to you always
 and until my last breath,
dear name, it will be yours." I'm back in the hospital room last night

 with my stroke-struck
father, who has forgotten how to talk, the right side of whose face
 sags and frowns.

He tries to whisper, "Wh, wh . . . ," but no word comes.
               Why, where,
what, when? He shrugs, half-smiles, shakes his head,

               and falls
silent. He looks at us with the unshuttable, glazed-over, gelid eyes
          of a king salmon

gutted and sold whole on crushed ice.
               I play another
record. With only the barest of orchestral accompaniment,

          violins feather-touched
and one sorrowing cello, the voice descends almost *a cappella.*
            Thy hand,

Belinda!   *Darkness shades me,*   *On thy bosom let me rest.*
          Then Purcell's aria
bursts forth, three reiterated lines that intertwine. *When I am laid,*

            am laid
in earth,   *May my wrongs create no trouble, no trouble*
            in thy breast!

Remember me, remember me.   *But ah, forget my fate.* The last "ah" of the aria
          gets held
for seven full seconds. "Remember me" haunts the score with its high Ds

          repeated six times.
An auburn-headed woman in denim shorts, whose tanned, water-smooth
          breasts are reined in

by a taupe velvet halter top, grimaces at the grainy sound
and asks me
what we're listening to. I tell her, "Flagstad. 'Dido's Lament.'"

"Who's that?"
she asks and wants to know if I can turn the volume up. I explain
that the Victor Talking

Machine Co.'s Victrola has only the one volume and that, for the best sound,
you have to sit
right in front of the speaker's wooden slats. She bends

sinuously
and brings one pink, perfectly spiraled, nautilus-shelled ear
down close

to Flagstad's voice. "It's better than nothing," she observes.
I want to tell her,
but don't, of course, that everything, all our poor living

and dying,
has been given voice by Flagstad in Purcell's Dido's long-held
"ah," that roller coaster

groan, triumphant sigh, post-orgasmic death swoon, swan song moan,
Remember me!   But ahhhhh,
forget my fate. My father in his mint-green johnny marked "Property

of Fairview Hospital,"
with a tan blanket around his bony wingless shoulders in place
of a penitent's

sackcloth cloak, shivers and sings his own slurred aria, "Hiz
        is nat slod
estion ober mard, but all zez fall in slall." He is king

        of aphasiacs,
a broken talking machine, to whom my mother and I bend close
        in homage

and listen hard, straining to catch one sentence, one phrase, one word
        of the man
we once knew. "Daddy," my mother interrupts, "do you remember

        your ambulance ride
today with me?" He shakes his head. She looks at him and then
        at me. "What

a bumpy ride! Next time I want something with shock absorbers.
        I want a limo.
No, next time I want a hearse!" She and I both laugh until we end up

        weeping.
When I am laid, am laid in earth. The 78 runs down, and the needle gets stuck
        on repeated

surf-like static. When I flip the record, the other side is blank except for
        the old trademark
of Angel Records, a staring Blakean cherub with half-folded wings

        who sits in the center
of a spinning disc on a turntable and draws grooves of sound
        in the black vinyl

with a feather pen as tall as he is. Is it the music of the spheres
          he transcribes,
nine rings of paradise from some celestial dictaphone,

          or the circles
of hell he draws around himself? The recording angel says only, "Listen
          well! Write what you hear."

My father taps his forehead and whispers slowly, "Zings nant . . .
          connect . . . sear. . . ."
Holding his cold hand in both of mine, I feel beneath my forefinger

          his pulse speed up,
the blood's shum-shum, the steel needle bearing down and stuck
          on seventy-eight

revolutions of silence per minute. Soon someone will lift the arm,
          push the lever,
and bring the whirling full-tilt turntable of the world to a dead stop.

Sundowning Exit-Seeker

Welcome to Geer
Memorial Nursing Home. Today is: Friday, August 16th, 2002.
        The next holiday is:

Labor Day. The season is: Summer. The weather is:
        Sunny & Hot—
"That's all you need to know," I tell my father and gesture jokingly

        toward the sign
on the wall of North Three, the nursing home's locked unit.
        It's after his supper

of fried chicken, vegetable medley, mashed potatoes with gravy,
        and chocolate pudding,
which my father ate with the back of his spoon. "Do you own

        this bit of real
estate?" Dad asks, motioning around the ward hung with Van Gogh's
        sunflowers. "How many

people live in this house? Can anyone tell me why I'm here?"
        I explain again
his stroke. "Oh, I see," he says, sighs, and doesn't see. Purple

        bruises splotch
both of his bare arms like Rorschachs, like black irises in late April,
        where the hospital nurses

tried to draw blood, but missed the veins. "Looks like they roughed
        you up good,"
Judy, the charge nurse, says. We all smile. A white-haired

          stooped woman
in a wheelchair tries to propel herself with slippered feet toward the wooden
           handrail that runs along the wall,

but she goes nowhere. Her frantic feet are bicycling a paddle boat.
          Dad gives her
a push so she can grip the rail and work her way

          slowly down
the hall, dragging herself along. "Your father's a sweet old guy,
          but stubborn,"

says Judy. "He turns off all the residents' air-conditioners,
          unplugs their TVs,
and winds up their alarm clocks. Last night he made it down

          the elevator
to the lobby and out the front door twice before security
          got him. He's

a very mobile exit-seeker, so we had to move him
          to the secure wing."
Judy winks at him. Dad grins. A black man in an armchair

          pulled out
into the hall wakes up and shouts, "What you doin' up so early?
          You don't have to go

to work now." A woman in nothing but a Mickey Mouse T-shirt
          too short
to cover her wrinkled thighs and balding pudendum's

few white wisps
holds out to Judy her soiled sweatpants and underwear.
              "It's all right,

Estelle," says Judy. "Juanita will take you back to your room
              and get you all
cleaned up." She turns to me, "Everyone here is

              sundowning."
When she sees that I don't understand, she adds, "Residents
              with dementia

often go bonkers in the late afternoon. No one knows why.
              They're fine
in the morning. We in the field call it 'sundowning.'"

              I see rows
on rows of Van Gogh's heavy-headed sunflowers turning their round, blank
              faces haloed

with golden manes toward the sun sinking over a field
              of unscythed hay.
Aren't we all phototropic? Or is my father's pale

              unshaven face,
from which I wipe a crusted glob of chocolate pudding,
              more a rare, night-blooming

orchid cactus that opens its white petals only to the darkness?
              He stands
and rearranges for hours the photographs and stuffed teddy bears

on his roommate's
dresser. They're never right, and he must move them a quarter inch
to left or right.

When I tell him I must go, he stops and says hopefully, "Good, then we
can go home together.
I'll pack my stuff. I'll only be a minute." I lie and tell him no,

not yet. The nurses
need to run more tests. His shoulders sag. Father, sundowning exit-seeker,
you'll leave here soon enough.

Name & Address

When I call my father long-distance on a Saturday night,
          he knows
my voice and doesn't need, as he did yesterday,

          to ask me
my name. He says, "Don, I'm in a bit of a jam." I hear him
          read from the creased

and greasy square of paper he folds and unfolds
          in his trembling
hands. "99 South Canaan Road, Canaan, Connecticut? Son,

          does that mean
anything to you?" "Yes, Dad, that's the address
          of the nursing home

where you live now." "Oh, so that's my new house!
          Well, I've got
to get on the road soon. Will there be anyone

          to help me
out there on the road and tell me which way to go
          to get back

home?" As I reassure him that his nurses will care
          for him, I remember
my mother printing my name, address, and telephone number

          on a scrap
of stationery and attaching it to my left breast pocket
          with a safety pin

before my first school field trip. I forget
                    where we went.
I was a letter she sent out into the unknown. I feel again

                    like a child
blindfolded at a birthday party and spun around and around
                    by large, unseen

hands, then released, and told to stumble forward and pin a strip
                    of paper to whatever
my hand first touches. "I've got to get out of here

                    and start hitchhiking
now," my father says. "Wish me luck." Crazily, dizzily, I want
                    to pin my father's

name and address on his soft night-blue flannel bathrobe so that
                    whatever road he travels
strangers will know what word to call him by

                    and what place
he has come from on his long journey through light and shadow
                    to the country of the deaf and dumb,

which is our only home. As my mother did for me once so long ago, I want
                    to kiss him lightly
on the forehead and let him go. "Goodbye, Daddy," I say. "Good luck."

Walt Whitman Wrestling Naked with the Young Trees

Every time I pass
the old sycamore on our corner, I touch its muscled
dappled torso

where the smooth flesh emerges from the bark's
rough scales.
Its branches drop on the ground their curled sheets

of old skin,
crumbled parchment or torn fine-grit sandpaper,
and where they were,

the secret greeny-white flesh shines. Today I saw
how one of its highest
boughs had been blown down across the sidewalk

by last night's
storm whose winds gusted over eighty miles per hour.
I stopped

and reached down to break off two of the twigs
with their three-pointed
maple-like leaves and examined the gash

where the limb
had been wrenched from its socket. Touching the ragged
splinters

of live wood wet with sap, I thought of
Walt Whitman
in 1877, after the two strokes that paralyzed

first the left,
then the right side of his body, and between them
the death of Louisa,

his mother. To heal his mind and fumbling
body, Whitman
at fifty-eight hobbled out to Timber

Creek, where he stripped
naked except for his boots and broad-brimmed
straw hat.

There he sunbathed and walked through "the stiff-
elastic bristles"
of chest-high weeds and bushes that "rasped arms, breast, sides

till they turn'd
scarlet." He then would wade into the creek and sink his feet
into the mud's

cool luxurious black ooze. Thus cleansed, every day
for two summers,
he wrestled hickory saplings naked, pulling down

the young trunks,
bending them into the shape of bows—his "natural gymnasia."
He swayed and yielded

to the "tough-limber upright stems," just as he wrestled
fully clothed
with Harry Stafford, the eighteen-year-old who helped to set

his book *Two Rivulets*
in type and who accepted his ring, then gave it back, then accepted
it again before

finally saying goodbye that summer. Those hickory saplings
and later beech
and holly boughs he bent until each muscle quivered

made him feel
"the sap and sinew rising" through him "like mercury
to heat."

Spanish moss–bearded father, you wrestled Harry and all those young trees
like Jacob
with his angel. Though you once pinned Harry

to the floor,
you couldn't pin the trees. They sprang back up
almost as straight

as they had been before they met you. They left you
old and broken.
Old man, it's you and my own life I touch

when I touch
the sycamore. Be whole again. Let your sap run through
the torn branch and into me.

After

After Orpheus returned from the high-rises of the dead,
        those catacombs
honeycombed with cold gray light, after Eurydice disappeared

        for good
in the subway crowded with shades and took the uptown local back
        to her pimp

Pluto, hung with gold chains, who beat her and sweet-talked her
        into bed,
Orpheus blinked in the sunlight, put on his ultra-cool

        mirror sunglasses,
and went back to work at the CD store, Tunes New, Used, & Abused.
        He moonlighted

as a rapper, played sax in the sultry mornings, and gave lyre lessons
        on the side.
His students brought him their odes and elegies, and he corrected

        the notes,
taught them the true arpeggios of desire, but he himself had sex
        with no one.

After Eurydice, he thought he might be gay and tried composing
        a few pastorals
for the handsome shepherd boys, who roamed the city parks,

        and got high with them
under the overpasses, but the notes fell flat. He rhymed
        buttocks with tux-

edos, and gave it up. He couldn't shake what he had seen
                    in the underworld,
his 85-year-old mother pushing the boulder up a steep off-ramp marked

                    Last Exit
Before Toll, only to have it roll back down into the oncoming
                    traffic, and then

to start all over again. He had seen his parched father chained
                    spread-eagled
to the top of a water tower and the vultures who visited

                    him daily
to eat his liver. His idiot brother had been bound to a Ferris wheel
                    of fire

that turned to the music of the One and Only Armenian-American
                    Polka Band.
What a carnival! Black cotton candy. And now Eurydice

                    wouldn't leave him
alone, but sent e-mails from hell, "I can't believe your savagery,"
                    etc., etc.

There was nothing else to do. He sat on a graffitied park bench,
                    fed the pigeons
Cracker Jacks, and unstrung his lyre. He swept his fingers

                    over the empty
space where the strings had been, and then there came that music
                    to which the stones and pigeons listened.

For Janis Joplin with Pink Feather Boa in the Clouds
at the Edge of the Atlantic Ocean

I'm listening to Janis
scream, croon, whine, caterwaul, claw, sob, kick, choke, stutter,
lullabye, and chainsaw

her way through Big Mama Thornton's "Ball and Chain,"
the live version
at the Monterey Pop Festival in June of 1967, on my Walkman's

headphones
as I'm running off my middle-aged baby fat, my three-mile
early morning run

on vacation alongside the big surf's one-man
percussion-and-brass
band. Janis wails to the crash of its thousand-pound

cymbals. Not even
the Atlantic Ocean can dwarf or drown that voice, diminish
in the crackling static

of its backwash her attack as she lets the coiled, razor-wire notes
escape
her throat—"Sittin' down by my window,

jus' lookin' out
at the rain." Her life was a long loneliness, one blink of eternity's
coquettish, gold-dusted

eyelashes, that no amount of smack and Southern Comfort, nor gorgeous
high-cheek-boned
Linda Gravenites who dressed her in greens and purples, silk bell-bottoms

and bangles, who washed
her dishes, could fill. She was always trying to leave Port Arthur, Texas.
"They laughed me out

of class, out of town, and out of the state—so I'm going home,"
she told
Dick Cavett. The fans scream and want to touch her electric

hair and the blue
tattooed bracelet on her left wrist. But who listens to Janis Joplin now
besides me? My kids

think I'm weird to fall hard in my mid-forties for this tough
blues mamma.
I know sincerity's not art, but listen to her vocal chords

tighten so she
can almost not get through the line, and half-shrieks, half-whispers,
"Honey, tell me why

why does everything go   go wrong   I say, honey, all gone wrong"
or how she phrases
that last sentence so it becomes not plea, but growled-out agony—"Come on

tell me   why   once in a while
oh baby, tell me why love   oh honey, why   why love is like
was like a ball

and a chain." Ah, that "a"! The difference one indefinite article
can make
is art. There's no one on the beach this morning except for a few fishermen

casting their lead weights
and snelled hooks baited with squid beyond the surf, and two or three
pairs of women

earnestly gossiping and walking together, kicking the foam
that is the ocean's
frothy underthings. They don't care that Janis Joplin lived

a fucked-up,
ecstatic, despairing life and died of booze and an overdose
of 50 percent-pure

heroin in the Landmark Hotel, L.A., almost thirty-one years ago
on the day before
she was supposed to go into the studio and lay down

the vocal track
for Nick Gravenites's new song, "Buried Alive in the Blues."
It's all rock 'n' roll

myth, and Janis has become no more than the few pink wisps
of a cirrus cloud's
feather boa half an hour after sunrise above the Atlantic's

surge and seethe.
Forget her lousy life. Let only this voice remain
coarse as a half-round

bastard wood rasp in a master craftsman's hand. I'm letting
her tremolo
in "Summertime   time   time" enter my backbone's

marrow
and shave and score the day until it's ground down
to pain and lust,

joy's hemidemisemiquaver. When she croons, "Nothing's goin'
to harm you now,"
she's rocking in her arms my three dead friends, gone within

the last
six months—a boy just hitting puberty head-on, a prime man
my age, and my uncle

in his eighty-third year—death's mother lode. She gnaws
and chews the sound
like fat red meat. The ocean's breakers are the bass line

over which she improvises
grace notes. I see fifty feet beyond the surf a school of dolphins surface.
They jump in arcs,

keystone arches that support the sky's groined dome.
Their black backs
flash golden in the morning sun. For half a minute

I'm running
with them, each of my strides matching their leaps, and all of us
moving in time

to the surf's two-stroke heartbeat, its redundant thunder. Then they dive
to the ocean's floor
and don't resurface. I run alone. Janis jokes two days before

she died, "I'd like to sing
a song of great social and political import. It goes like this . . ." and then
she's off *a cappella* in her last

chorus, one ringed hand banging out the beat on a flimsy beer crate,
"Everybody . . .
Lord, won't you buy me a Mercedes Benz," those final words held long

and trilled, kissed lingeringly
goodbye, before she switches to her everyday, wisecracking voice—
"That's it!"—and laughs.

Pretty Boy, Rifle Barrels, Carnations

Do you remember
the photograph of war protesters in front of the Pentagon,
1967, how the MPs

have raised their rifles until they're level with the chests
of the crowd?
And how one eighteen-year-old boy with dirty-blond hair

in a ribbed, roll-neck
sweater is carefully placing carnations stem-first into the small
dark mouths

of the rifles? That gesture caught on a photojournalist's
35-millimeter film
seemed so spontaneous it became the symbol

of a whole generation's
rebellion, their daydream that M-16 rifles might blossom
and shoot

petals, not bullets. It became "flower power," mere cliché.
Look again.
That bouquet of carnations clutched in the war protester's

damp left palm
is starting to wilt and must have been purchased for this
express purpose.

The flowers are premeditated, a bit of agitprop.
The pretty boy,
who has squeezed lemon juice all summer into his hair

on Jones Beach
to bleach it, is a young stage actor named George Harris,
traveling from

New York to San Francisco, where he will become
within three years
Hibiscus, cross-dressing, high-kicking star of the Cockettes,

gay troupe
that mounted such productions as "Journey to the Center
of Uranus"

and "Tinsel Tarts in a Hot Coma." Hibiscus grew
a beard
that he sprinkled with gold glitter and wore false

inch-long eyelashes.
A friend said, "He came out of the closet, wearing the entire
closet." He had

"an extraordinary way with old kimonos, torn gowns,
lace, glitter,
and wilting flora." He would be dead from AIDS by 1982

at thirty-three.
Isn't that trajectory contained in the war-protester photograph
so that it's really

more about sex than politics? See how gently George inserts
each green stem
into the rifle barrel so it will jet a spray of white carnations,

those flesh flowers,
like globs of warm come toward his full, welcoming lips. He'd already
had several

lovers. And aren't the MPs just kids in their early twenties,
barely older
than George? They stare in disbelief, not anger,

at this younger brother
with his preppy haircut and hothouse flowers. One reaches out
and touches

with amazement the carnations sprouting from his friend's
rifle. Sure,
the next moment he'll yank them out, throw them

to the ground,
and grind them into the asphalt with the heel of his dress-parade
boot. The MPs'

helmets are phallic, the heads of circumcised hard-ons.
They are so shiny
each helmet reflects the same two trees and the northern

corner of the Pentagon,
behind which the late August sun is setting. Here politics, war, and sex
intersect

so it's impossible to separate one from the others. 1969, the year
after the Tet offensive,
when the film footage of a Vietnamese woman on fire with napalm

running away
from her bombed-out village was confiscated as "anti-American
propaganda," I was

twelve and masturbating over the luxurious buttocks
of Eve
in Michelangelo's *Fall of Man* from the Sistine Chapel.

Hibiscus
was doing the cancan in a grass skirt, wearing the top halves
of pineapples

for breasts and had a nose-ring and bunches of grapes and lavender orchids
twined in his glittered
hair. He was the Dionysus of Drag, American hermaphrodite.

Aren't we all,
gay or straight or somewhere in-between, trying to recover
our lost bodies,

our other half? But what about the napalmed woman
who wore
a shirt of fire she couldn't take off? George Harris

alias Hibiscus
will keep silencing the mouths of rifles so they speak nothing
but fresh-cut carnations.

Setting Sun

If you looked at the setting sun on a November Sunday in 1944
　　　　　from a tarred rooftop
in New York City between the lines of washing hung

　　　　　　　out to dry
like flags of surrender, would you too see what Eugenie Baizerman,
　　　　　　　née Silverman,

saw and set down in the raw pigments of vermilion and burnt sienna
　　　　　　　on two canvas panels,
each four-and-a-half by three-and-a-half feet, because she didn't

　　　　　　have one piece
of canvas already stretched and sized and big enough?
　　　　　　Her painting is all

flames twisting up from a bonfire that roars, splutters, and spits
　　　　　　　back at us.
An arc welder's shower of sparks. Then I see

　　　　　　that those flames
are six naked women. One cups her right molten breast in her right
　　　　　　palm. Another

gathers her hair and coils it into a bun. One scrubs
　　　　　　her left thigh
with a blazing sponge. Another twists her torso and raises

　　　　　　both arms above
her head as if about to dive into a pool of cool water.
　　　　　　One crosses

her arms and waits. Another turns and walks away
                from us
with the smooth, strong-muscled, burnished calves that only

                young women have.
All six of them are burning. They do what women everywhere
                do every day,

but they are a frieze of fire. Eugenie Baizerman looked
                into the setting
sun and saw them there with her terrified

                prophetic
squinting eyes. Within the next nine months how many bodies would
                blaze out in the firestorm's

vortex? It reached 1600 degrees centigrade and sucked up
                all available
oxygen, so that even those who huddled together in the underground

                shelters
often suffocated. Many were refugees. It is impossible to calculate ashes
                with any accuracy.

They have vanished into the names of cities. Dresden, Tokyo,
                Hiroshima—
our shorthand for catastrophe. Those who survived the firestorm

                crowded the roads
out of Dresden and were "routinely strafed" by P-51D Mustangs.
                What Baizerman knew

is that the Pentecostal apocalyptic fire will take us
            when we least
expect it, when we're eating an apple, playing hopscotch,

            washing our hands.
It will teach us to speak in new tongues, which have always
            been ours

though we didn't know it. In the photo essay, a charred child
            clutches its charred
mother around her waist. Their eyeless faces are those of Baizerman's

            six naked women
and have been peeled away like the rinds of blood oranges. Photographs
            of war are pure

pornography. But Saul, Baizerman's sculptor husband,
            would have said
that Eugenie was no oracle, that she was just remembering

            "glowing fruits
and flowers, nude women bathing in the Black Sea" at sunset near Odessa
            where her father,

a linguistics professor, and her Jewish mother, an amateur actress,
            encouraged her
to study art. But there's the date, 1944. And isn't art, like it or not,

            an eyewitness
to what it can't see and to what, if it could see,
            would blind us?

Baizerman's six women are condemned to stand forever,
              robed in the royal
roiling flames of their own flesh. Not one hair

              of their blazoned heads
shall be harmed. They are Shadrach, Meschach, and Abednego singing
              to their god upon a ten-stringed

harp of fire. But when the furnace doors are opened on the last day
              the women of Tokyo,
Dresden, and Hiroshima and all their children shall not come forth.

Snapshot

Tomorrow is my father's
eighty-seven birthday. He walks the halls of his nursing home's locked unit
in pink pajamas,

refuses to bathe, get dressed, or shave. In the end even the immortals
become
mortal. In the next-to-last snapshot I have of my father

before his stroke,
he stands in black slacks and white short-sleeved shirt
in front of a birch tree

by our summer house. The light touches
the left side
of his face and body and leaves the other half in shadow.

The birch tree
is the same color as my father. Shouldn't we shut
our eyes to keep

death out? My father stares straight into the camera.
Father, close
your eyes. Touch the tattered flesh

of the birch,
its smooth bark starting to peel off in strips. My mother will thumb
shut your eyelids, wrinkled

as fallen star magnolia petals. Eyes closed, I hold again your thin right arm
where a butterfly-shaped scar
has settled above the elbow. I must trace its white wings.

Andantino Cantabile with Double Rainbow

I keep listening
to the allegro, the third movement of Mozart's piano concerto in E-flat
on endless repeat

through scattered rain squalls, windshield wipers like metronomes,
while driving back
to my mother's house after a visit with my father in the nursing

home. The piano slows
to a few notes dripping from a faucet someone's forgotten to turn off,
and I'm in a different tempo,

time, and key. The woodwinds take up a somber-timbred theme
in A-flat major,
three-quarter time. Now the piano's notes are

lemon, vermilion, ocher—
autumn leaves falling from a grove of sugar maples into accumulating
silence. The tempo

is *andantino cantabile,* meaning "a little faster than moderately
slow, flowingly
and in a singing style." I stop to pump gas

at a Mobil station,
an old-fashioned one which still has a red-winged horse
flying across

a blue stucco wall as its logo. It's "full serve."
A man with *Mike*
stitched in white across his gray work shirt's left breast pocket

ambles over
to "fill her up." Through the rolled-down window my nostrils flare
with the thin, intoxicating

smell of spilled gasoline. Mike (though he could be Joe or Jim for all
I know and just wearing
Mike's soiled shirt) suddenly stops pumping and points

at the sky. I
hop out. Cars are swerving off the highway onto the shoulder. The sun
has broken through. Couples,

single drivers, whole bickering families of six to eight kids spill out
of their cars, station wagons,
or minivans like some circus act. Everyone is looking up

and pointing.
"Never seen anything like it in my entire life!" says Mike (or Jim or Joe).
"Wow, it really is

in Technicolor, just like on the Disney channel," observes one precocious
six-year-old.
The mother of all rainbows arcs from horizon to

horizon, connecting
the humpbacked, watermelon mountains to our near
valley. It arcs

in chords of color, six clear notes, three-quarters of an ascending
diatonic scale,
A-flat major. Purple shading into blue, then green,

re mi fa,
yellow going up the staff from orange into red, *so la ti.*
No, it's a full

spectrum's octave with sky-blue *do*'s on either side
for high and low
notes, heaven's tonics. Part of another rainbow,

only a shattered
thirty-degree arc, shadows the full rainbow, hovering over
its rim—like an imperfect

echo—from one to two o'clock. How is it that my one small impoverished life
contains, *andantino*
cantabile, these miles of rain, sun, such double rainbows, and the greasy rag

that Mike (it must be
Mike!) wipes his hands on after he's finished pumping gas? It flutters
like a flag

from his left back pocket. I keep seeing the manacle-like bruises around
my father's wrists,
where the orderlies have had to hold him down for his weekly shower.

The contused skin is umber,
yellow, mauve, and black. Around his wrists he wears dark rainbows
that hold him to the earth.

Cartwheels

That truly the body is a wheel
            in perpetual
motion, that it was never meant

                to stand
upright on two flat feet rooted
            firmly

to the ground, but instead
                to bend
sapling-supple at the waist and hurl

                itself down
and sideways so that the limbs
                spread out

like a starfish's arms from the hub
            of the solar
plexus and become spokes

                that connect
to an invisible
                circumference,

rim that keeps rolling
            the body
around our living room,

                    is the
        unlikely theorem that my daughter
                  proves over

        and over. But how long
              it took her
        to master the cartwheel's

                  fluid
        geometry, days, weeks
              of flailing

        legs, bruised knees, palms
                  burning, her
        torso wobbling and toppling

                  into
        a tangle of limbs! But then
              that moment

        when the body, which had been
                a teetering
        top, suddenly came

                into true
        and the center of balance
              shifted

        a few millimeters and she
                  was
        cartwheeling our worn

kitchen
linoleum, where I stooped
         scrubbing

the crusted dishes and sighing
         over my dying
parents as she

         showed me another
way of walking
         this weighted world.

Amazing Grace Beauty Salon

Because walk-ins are welcome
at the Amazing Grace Beauty Salon, I go in out of the August
sun, let my unkempt

self be wrapped in a purple plastic winding sheet,
and am baptized
without ceremony by Elaine, who plunges my head

three times under
the hot faucet in the name of shampoo, conditioner, and once more
for good luck.

I breathe the holy mysteries of stinky beauty potions and listen to the Muzak
of this sphere, her shears
twittering as they wing through air. "Just you lay back, honey."

Let the voices of women
envelop and uplift me so that my mind floats free and drifts
on the great mothering

waters of sound. "My Doug, he's fixin' to buy a hot-pink suit.
He'll do it too!
That man don't care what anyone thinks."

It's small talk, the heart's
murmur, a slow delta river. Elaine swaps stories with Delaine, a black woman
whose shuttling fingers braid

abalone shells into a young girl's cornrows. Delaine replies, "Why I seen him
in his purple suit
with that yellow shirt, an' I tell him he look like a bumblebee.

I tell him
he look like a Easter egg." "Nah," says Elaine, "he looks like
a bag of Skittles."

"Go on," Delaine shoots back, setting a timer for someone's
perm. "Why, I
tell him he look like he's black." Silence, then nervy laughter.

Elaine catches her breath
and explains, in case I don't get it, "Black people like bright colors.
My Doug, he's a very

colorful character." She smiles shyly at her own sly
pun. Here
is history squeezed into the silence between two jokes—years

that are mile-long
rows of cumulus cotton to be picked by black fingers, husks that cut,
Emmett Till carrying

on his back the 75-pound cotton-gin fan, lashed
with barbed wire
to his neck, across the ruts of the night field

to the Tallahatchie River,
where the two white men ordered him to strip by flashlight, gouged out
one eye, shot

him in the head, and stomped him good before throwing to the sluggish
silted current
his corpse, this fourteen-year-old Chicago boy who "done the talkin'",

who stuttered "Bye, Baby"
on a dare to the pretty white woman at Bryant's Grocery & Meat Market
in Money, Mississippi.

History is a river, so Isaac Watts once hymned. It floods its banks each spring.
It carries budding cottonwoods
pulled up like wisdom teeth by their roots, deer carcasses, empty fifty-five gallon

oil drums, whatever floats and whatever
doesn't. It carries us all. The Tallahatchie still holds Emmett Till's body
and will never wash it clean,

but bloats it so that his grandfather doesn't recognize him
and knows him only
by an initialed silver ring. These floodwaters overflow the casual

conversation of two
women passing the time while cutting hair, black body, white body,
Delaine, Elaine,

names that keep switching places in my head. Delaine tells the story
of her father
going to Big Jeff's Barber Shop on the square

in Americus, Georgia,
1963. Dressed in his Sunday best, a pink seersucker suit, he swaggered in
and half-asked, half-announced,

"Do y'all cut nigger hair?" Big Jeff, two-hundred-eighty-pound
ex-Marine stropping a razor
like strumming a guitar, didn't miss a chord. "I never cut

no nigger's hair
and ain't about to start now." Thirty-seven years later, everyone in the salon
quits talking. "When Daddy wouldn't

leave without his haircut, Big Jeff slashed him bad." Elaine puts her hand
on Delaine's bare shoulder.
She shrugs it off. "They're both dead now. I styled my daddy's hair

when they laid him out.
It done turned pure white. He always was a headstrong, handsome man."
Hair grows. It must be cut.

"Finish him, will you? I got a manicure to do." Delaine takes a palmful
of mousse and runs her fingers hard
through my hair, those fingers that groom all of us, the living and the dead.

Two Poets Meet

for Carlos Drummond de Andrade
and Elizabeth Bishop

When my two favorite poets in the whole infinitely worded world met,
and they met
only once, it was by chance on the sidewalk at night in Rio,

and they had just come out
of the same restaurant, where they had eaten at separate tables. Drummond
had had the humble tutu,

black beans mixed with manioc meal, and fried bananas. Elizabeth the gringa
had wolfed down
a caper and pimento picadinho served with farofa, manioc farina larded

with butter, sausage,
and eggs. Both had drunk cachaça with chasers of beer. The acacias
were in full bloom

and lit the street with their yellow globes. Their faint scent
could not conceal
the smell of urine from the side alley where the drunks would piss

copiously and with great
long-winded sighs. The panhandlers were out with their chorus of coughs
and por favors.

Lota, who knew everybody, introduced them. Elizabeth had not yet
started to translate
Drummond's verse. Drummond had never read any of Elizabeth's

few poems, which shone like a single
strand of pearls against a black funeral dress. Because they were both
"supposed to be very shy,"

they said little and spoke only the formalities
in Portuguese,
which was Elizabeth's third, half-learned language.

But when Lota
had taken Drummond's arm and whispered that there was someone
he must meet,

he was anything but gauche. He bent over Elizabeth's
outstretched
hand and put his lips, which had once murmured, "Love in the dark,

no, love
in the daylight, is always sad," briefly to the dry skin
of the back of her hand.

Let it be recorded that in the life where people meet and pass
there was a kiss
in the middle of a sidewalk. In the middle of the sidewalk, this kiss.

Red Door

How handsome my father
still is in that wallet-sized photo my 88-year-old mother
keeps by

the telephone! His thick black hair is parted on the left
and combed diagonally
to the right, so that it catches the light from the studio's

umbrella lamps
and glistens. He smiles wide. His cheeks rise. His large black eyes
gaze out

with a look meant only for my mother. He is dressed to kill
in his khaki
army shirt with a neatly knotted black tie and a small

gold cross
pinned to his collar, which means he's a chaplain in the Seabees
about to be sent

to Saipan and Okinawa, 1944. This is the man my mother first
met on the morning bus
to Santa Monica. She was answering an ad for a "room to let"

in a boarding house.
He had a day of leave and wanted to take a swim in the Pacific, stretch out
on his towel and watch

the pale-legged girls stroll by the mumbling surf. The two glanced shyly
at each other.
When they both boarded the evening bus back to L.A., they started talking.

Three weeks later they got married,
had a champagne breakfast with friends at her boarding house. Next morning
he shipped out. Sixty years

hurl by like bumper-to-bumper cars at 70 mph on the L.A. freeway.
My mother visits
my father on North Three, the nursing home's locked unit, every day.

Though he's forgotten
everyone else, he still remembers her. She kisses him full on his purple-blue lips,
which look as if

he's been drinking grape Kool-Aid on the sly.
It's his poor
circulation. When they kiss, his watery, hooded

lizard eyes
wake and glint for a moment like those of the young man in the photograph.
"Do you remember,"

she asks, "how we went all over England, France, and Italy on our
motorcycle?
Coventry, Carcassonne, Vézalay, Rome?" Those names brim

in her mouth, turn
to honeycomb. He shakes his head no. "We would go where the cars
couldn't. When the steep

cobblestone streets became stairs, we rode up the smooth gutters
on the sides.
Don't you remember?" He grins lopsidedly as if to apologize

for his stroke.

"It took you four years to finish your doctoral thesis on the first one hundred
years of the Church of England,

two volumes, one thousand sixty-four pages, with nineteen appendices!
You wrote about Jewel, Hooker,
Andrews, and Laud. Your tutor was Norman Sykes. He must be

dead now. But aren't
they all? That's history for you!" The three of us laugh
uncomfortably.

Suddenly my mother points to the watercolor on the wall.
She painted it
fifty-four years ago. It shows a woman with a child

walking by
a bright red door on a narrow English street. "That's where we used
to live. Remember

Number Two, Little St. Mary's Lane? The red door? The park? Our church?"
My father hesitates,
but only for a second, then says, "Of course I do. Who can forget

our red door?"
My mother smiles. I want to say that the past and the future are
a door like fire

we must walk through forward and backwards. Time is a room
we rent
by an ocean that fills our ears with the surf's susurrus and lamentation

morning, noon,
and night. We live and die in it. The lease is day-to-day. The small photograph
my mother keeps

by the telephone, on which my father will never call her again, is no illusion.
He always smiles
back at her. He is about to say something only she

hears. Their years together
are the morning bus, the evening bus. "Though you forget it all," she replies,
"that's what happened!"

Ground Transport

Above the clouds, the weather
is always clear, sunlight's glare off the leading edge of the 757's wings,
endless blue

of the sky's glass dome cupped over us, cloud cover stretching
like vast snow fields
below us or heavy cream whipped until the soft peaks start

to form, nothing
to stop the eye from traveling to infinity, horizon's ring of lighter
dirty blue

around the sky's cerulean bathtub. Who drew the clouds'
luxurious bubble bath
through whose foam I catch occasional glimpses of the Rockies'

wrinkled knees?
Nobody I know. To get here we had to climb thirty-five thousand feet,
leaving behind

our grounded lives, the city like a computer's motherboard hardwired
with sunlight,
the sinuous letters that a river carves in cursive through the farmland's

field painting,
palette of greens and earth tones, an abstract masterpiece, all the mistakes
and revisions showing through,

a copper mine's raw umbers daubed and scraped away
as if by Diebenkorn
in his *Ocean Park* series or some other great abstract expressionist

with a whole lot of nothing
still to express. Down there, six miles below us, the friend I visited
        continues

with her day, makes peanut-butter-and-strawberry-jam sandwiches
            ("much better
than raspberry"), takes her three kids to school, works,

            works out, cooks
potato frittatas, naps, all without the husband who one and a half years ago
            had a manic

break and left them for a Ferrari and a cattle ranch in Arizona. He won't
        take his meds.
On their way home, stuck in gridlocked traffic, her youngest daughter

        will point
to the sunset and say, "Look, Mom, the sky is tie-dyed gold and blue!"
        They will gaze up

and stare at slabs of clouds that turn to pink-veined Tuscan marble
        and then to the flesh
of pomegranates ground beneath some hobnailed heel, the whole western

        horizon smeared with light.
For that one moment they will forget all loneliness, grief, and anger
        and feel themselves

dissolve and enter this cold luminescence that doesn't touch them
        but washes away
the sky in its river of rush-hour fire. Isn't it oblivion,

the sunset's golden
obituary, night's blackout, the Beatles' numbing, thought-obliterating
"ob-la-di, ob-la-da"

that we hunger for? Or is it rather transport, to step outside
our halting
bodies, to be "carried across," away, out, toward, back into

some new country
where the soul improvises, croons scat to itself alone, and is its own
mother and father,

helpmate, wife and husband? Ezra Pound, sprung from the steel-mesh
open-air birdcages
at Pisa, magpie with no shelter from sun or hail, extradited

to stand trial
for treason in the States, flew for the first time and walked the aisles
of a U.S. Army

transport plane, singing. What tune he belted out over the doom drone
of a DC-4's
propellers and the turbulence of low-pressure air pockets

above the Atlantic
is not recorded. He sang himself sane. A mountain range of cumulus
accumulates

on the horizon above the horizon. The flight attendants serve biscotti
and, for a price,
vodka on ice. My neighbor sleeps his way across

the continent,
head thrown back, mouth open. What dreams are gargling at the back
of his throat?

Will they take root in the clouds' topsoil? Will they grow
in this petri dish
of perpetual sunlight above the storm front's bruised, violet

violence?
I remember seeing Georgia O'Keeffe's *Sky Above Clouds,* eight by twenty-four
feet, painted

when she was seventy-eight. It is an old woman's out-of-body vision,
soul's levitation
to a place without gravity. The clouds are stepping stones that lead across

a wide blue river
straight to sunrise. She had to paint quickly before the cold weather set in.
The canvas was so large

that she later said, "As I worked I could walk back long distances out
onto the plain behind the garage
to look at what I was doing." She added that "the big painting

with its cool light
looked quite wonderful from almost any distance—even from a quarter
of a mile." Isn't

distance what we want? To be lifted up out of our dailiness,
to let our lives
diminish to the size of toy houses, dice thrown across

a green-and-russet-checkered
game-board, then vanish, to be suspended for one and three-quarter hours
        of flight time in the ether's

azure, its shining emptiness? We must descend. The plane goes down
                through the low
cloud cover, and we are lost and muffled in gray

                wet cotton
batting. When the ground appears, it's suddenly only three hundred feet
        below us.

First, a swamp with cattails, then the soy beans' yards and yards
                of dark green
cambric spread flat upon a table to be measured

                out and cut, a full
parking lot, and then the landing strip scrawled with zebra zigzags
                and yellow lines to guide

us in. "Bare ground, bare ground," my brother used to chant
                ecstatically,
relieved when the wheels touched down. "Welcome to Indianapolis,"

                the lead flight attendant
croons. "Thank you for traveling Northwest with us." The day
                is overcast.

Next week my eighty-five-year-old mother will be going under
                general anesthesia
to have "something on an ovary" removed. There are papers

to be signed.
I will walk along the moving walkway to claim my baggage and continue on
            into what's left of the late

daylight. I will follow the black-and-white signs that say to all of us travelers
            not "Come unto me
all ye that travail," but only "This Way to Ground Transport."